WITH

34.99 ﬨ/יﬨ)יﬡ

MARQUIS

Marquis Book Printing Inc.

Québec, Canada
2010

EAT THESE WORDS

A Delicious Collection of Fat-free Food for Thought

Edited by Michael Cader
& Debby Roth

Illustrated by Lonni Sue Johnson

HarperCollins Publishers

Created by Cader Books, 24 West 10th Street, New York, NY 10011

FIRST EDITION

Designer: *Michael Cader*

Library of Congress Cataloging-in-Publication Data

Eat these words : a delicious collection of fat-free food for thought
  / edited by Michael Cader & Debby Roth : illustrated by Lonni Sue
Johnson. — 1st ed.
      p.   cm.
   ISBN 0-06-016633-9
   1. Quotations, English.   2. Food—Quotations, maxims, etc.
3. Food—Humor.   I. Cader, Michael, 1961–   . II. Roth, Debby,
1934–   .
PN 6084.F6E38   1991
641.3—dc20   90-55923

---

91 92 93 94 95   HC   10 9 8 7 6 5 4 3 2 1

Contents

The Four Basic Food-for-Thought Groups

Frustration..........11

Energy Conservation......49

Shame.......71

Love.......101

Man does not live by words alone, despite the fact that sometimes he has to eat them.

ADLAI STEVENSON

Where do you go to get anorexia?

SHELLEY WINTERS

It's not what you would call a figure, is it?

TWIGGY

Never practice two vices at once.

TALLULAH BANKHEAD

I was always eager to salt a good stew. The trouble was that I was expected to supply the meat and potatoes as well.

BETTE DAVIS

The whole of nature, as has been said, is a conjugation of the verb to eat, in the active and the passive.

WILLIAM RALPH INGE

One cannot think well, love well, sleep well, if one has not dined well.

VIRGINIA WOOLF

It is nonsense to speak of "higher" and "lower" pleasures. To a hungry man it is, rightly, more important that he eat than that he philosophize.

W. H. AUDEN

Avoid restaurants with names that are improbable descriptions, such as the Purple Goose, the Blue Kangaroo or the Quilted Orangutan.

CALVIN TRILLIN

Music with dinner is an insult both to the cook and the violinist.

G. K. CHESTERTON

I eat merely to put food out of my mind.

N. F. SIMPSON

I can reason down or deny everything except this perpetual belly: feed he must and will, and I cannot make him respectable.

RALPH WALDO EMERSON

Principles have no real force except when one is well fed.

MARK TWAIN

I'm tired of all this nonsense about beauty being only skin-deep. That's deep enough. What do you want, an adorable pancreas?

RITA MAE BROWN

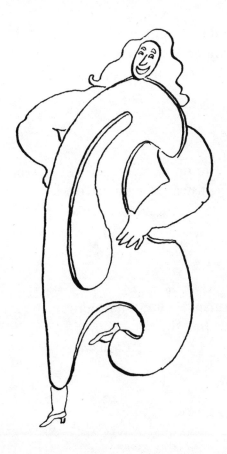

An optimist is a girl who mistakes a bulge for a curve.

RING LARDNER

All people are made alike—
of bones and flesh and dinner—
Only the dinners are different.

GERTRUDE LOUISE CHENEY

I would like to find a stew that will give me heartburn
immediately, instead of at three o'clock in the morning.

JOHN BARRYMORE

An Englishman teaching an American about food is like
the blind leading the one-eyed.

A. J. LIEBLING

A gourmet is just a glutton with brains.

PHILIP HABERMAN, JR.

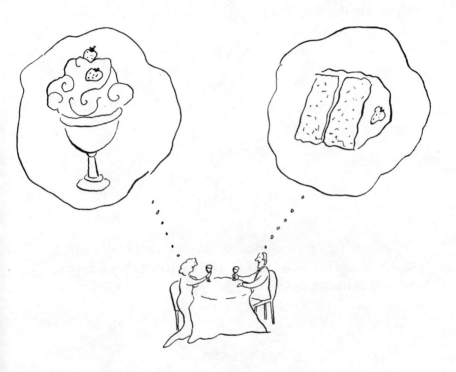

Man is the only animal, I believe, who pretends he is
thinking of other things while he is eating.

ROBERT LYND

There is no dignity in the bean. Corn, with no affectation of superiority, is, however the child of song. It waves in all literature. But mix it with beans and its high tone is gone. Succotash is vulgar.

CHARLES DUDLEY WARNER

Abstain from beans.

PLUTARCH

Inhabitants of undeveloped nations and victims of natural disasters are the only people who have ever been happy to see soybeans.

FRAN LEBOWITZ

You can travel fifty thousand miles in America without once tasting a piece of good bread.

HENRY MILLER

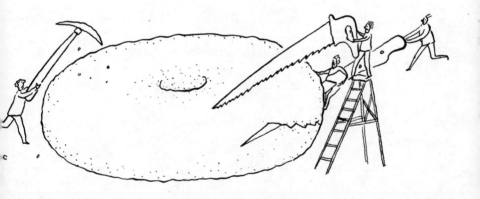

The bagel, an unsweetened doughnut with rigor mortis . . .

BEATRICE & IRA FREEMAN

Bouillabaisse is only good because it is cooked by the French, who if they cared to try, would produce an excellent and nutritious substitute out of cigar stumps and empty matchboxes.

NORMAN DOUGLAS

You are better off not knowing how sausages and laws are made.

UNKNOWN

The trouble with eating Italian food is that five or six days later you're hungry again.

GEORGE MILLER

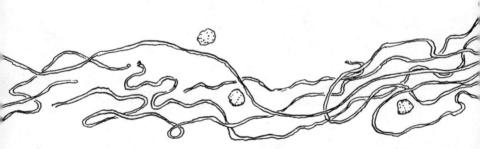

I will not eat oysters. I want my food dead—not sick, not wounded—dead.

WOODY ALLEN

In Mexico we have a word for sushi: bait.

JOSÉ SIMON

Should I stop swatting flies? Should I invite mice into my kitchen and serve them lunch? This speciesism is specious.

JULIA CHILD

I am human. I eat meat.

GILBERT LE COZE

I want nothing to do with natural foods. At my age I need all the preservatives I can get.

GEORGE BURNS

It's no longer a question of staying healthy. It's a question of finding a sickness you like.

JACKIE MASON

Health Food: The food they serve in Hell.

HENRY BEARD

If you have formed the habit of checking on every new diet that comes along, you will find, mercifully, they all blur together, leaving you with only one definite piece of information: french-fried potatoes are out.

JEAN KERR

It's okay to be fat. So you're fat. Just be fat and shut up about it.

ROSEANNE BARR

Beauty does not season soup.

POLISH PROVERB

Attention to health is life's greatest hindrance.

PLATO

Health food makes me sick.

CALVIN TRILLIN

I am not a glutton—I am an explorer of food.

ERMA BOMBECK

The two biggest sellers in any bookstore are the cookbooks and the diet books. The cookbooks tell you how to
prepare the food and the diet books tell you how not to
eat any of it.

ANDY ROONEY

I'm not going to starve to death just so I can live a little
longer.

IRENE PETER

Quit worrying about your health. It'll go away.

ROBERT ORBEN

I have no truck with lettuce, cabbage, and similar chloro-phyll. Any dietician will tell you that a running foot of apple strudel contains four times the vitamins of a bushel of beans.

S. J. PERELMAN

Vegetarianism is harmless enough, though it is apt to fill a man with wind and self-righteousness.

SIR ROBERT HUTCHINSON

Vegetarian: A person who eats only side dishes.

GERALD LIEBERMAN

Vegetarians have wicked, shifty eyes, and laugh in a cold calculating manner.

J. B. MORTON

Never order anything in a vegetarian restaurant that would ordinarily have meat in it.

TOM PARKER

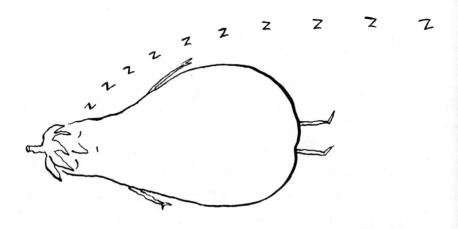

Vegetables are interesting but lack a sense of purpose when unaccompanied by a good cut of meat.

FRAN LEBOWITZ

I'm not a vegetarian because I love animals; I'm a vegetarian because I hate plants.

A. WHITNEY BROWN

Parsley
Is gharshley.

OGDEN NASH

Large, naked raw carrots are acceptable as food only to those who lie in hutches eagerly awaiting Easter.

FRAN LEBOWITZ

I say it's spinach, and I say the hell with it.

E. B. WHITE

(On nouvelle cuisine) It's so beautifully arranged on the plate—you know someone's fingers have been all over it.

JULIA CHILD

I've been on a diet for two weeks and all I've lost is two weeks.

TOTIE FIELDS

On liquid diet fad: The powder is mixed with water and tastes exactly like powder mixed with water.

ART BUCHWALD

Don't eat too many almonds. They add weight to the breasts.

COLETTE

Some people like to eat octopus. Liberals, mostly.

RUSSELL BAKER

Life is too short to stuff a mushroom.
SHIRLEY CONRAN

Eat as much as you like—just don't swallow it.
STEVE BURNS

There is a charm about the forbidden that makes it unspeakably desirable.
MARK TWAIN

Terrible is the temptation to be good!
BERTOLT BRECHT

I can resist everything but temptation.
OSCAR WILDE

Lead me not into temptation; I can find the way myself.

RITA MAE BROWN

Things taste better in small houses.

QUEEN VICTORIA

If fresh broccoli is not cooked properly, then it becomes a big ugly thing, and I don't think any little kiddie or any big President would like it.

JULIA CHILD

My grandmother would cook broccoli until it was mush. But she wouldn't let a Republican get away with this . . . . He simply must taste fresh broccoli cooked properly.

JEFF SMITH

You can't make broccoli exciting. You have to suffer when you eat it. It's disgusting, but I love it.

BRIAN MCNALLY

I do not like broccoli, and I haven't liked it since I was a little kid and my mother made me eat it. And I'm President of the United States, and I'm not going to eat any more broccoli.

GEORGE BUSH

The food here is so tasteless you could eat a meal of it and belch and it wouldn't remind you of anything.

REDD FOXX

There is one thing more exasperating than a wife who can cook and won't and that's a wife who can't cook and will.

ROBERT FROST

I never see any home cooking. All I get is fancy stuff.

DUKE OF EDINBURGH

As a child my family's menu consisted of two choices: take it, or leave it.

BUDDY HACKETT

The most remarkable thing about my mother is that for thirty years she served the family nothing but leftovers. The original meal has never been found.

CALVIN TRILLIN

Men do not have to cook their food; they do so for symbolic reaons to show they are men and not beasts.

EDMUND LEACH

Even the finest of cookbooks is no substitute for the poorest of dinners.

ALDOUS HUXLEY

Bad cooks—and the utter lack of reason in the kitchen— have delayed human development longest and impaired it most.

FRIEDRICH NIETZSCHE

An ill cook should have a good cleaver.

ENGLISH PROVERB

Murder is commoner among cooks than among members of any other profession.

W. H. AUDEN

It takes some skill to spoil a breakfast—even the English can't do it.

JOHN KENNETH GALBRAITH

To eat well in England you should have breakfast three times a day.

SOMERSET MAUGHAM

In England there are sixty different religions, but only one sauce.

VOLTAIRE

Coffee in England is just toasted milk.

CHRISTOPHER FRY

A cucumber should be well-sliced, dressed with pepper and vinegar, and then thrown out, as good for nothing.

Samuel Johnson

I feel about airplanes the way I feel about diets. It seems to me they are wonderful things for other people to go on.

JEAN KERR

I told my doctor I get very tired when I go on a diet, so he gave me pep pills. Know what happened? I ate faster.

JOE E. LEWIS

I've run more risk eating my way across the country than in all my driving.

DUNCAN HINES

A definition of eternity: A ham and two people.

IRMA S. ROMBAUER & MARION ROMBAUER BECKER

Eternity is two people and a roast turkey.

JAMES DENT

The murals in restaurants are on a par with the food in museums.

PETER DE VRIES

Water taken in moderation cannot hurt anybody.

MARK TWAIN

Ask your child what he wants for dinner only if he's buying.

FRAN LEBOWITZ

I asked the clothing store clerk if she had anything to make me look thinner, and she said, "How about a week in Bangladesh?"

ROSEANNE BARR

Once, during Prohibition, I was forced to live for days on nothing but food and water.

W. C. FIELDS

I stay in marvelous shape. I worry it off.
NANCY REAGAN

If you want to look young and thin, hang around old fat people.
JIM EASON

I'm Jewish. I don't work out. If God wanted us to bend over he'd put diamonds on the floor.
JOAN RIVERS

There's a great new rice diet that always works—you use one chop stick.
RED BUTTONS

When I was forty, my doctor advised me that a man in his forties shouldn't play tennis. I heeded his advice carefully and could hardly wait until I reached fifty to start again.

HUGO BLACK

⟨⟨═⟨⟩

When men reach their sixties and retire, they go to pieces. Women go right on cooking.

GAIL SHEEHY

⟨⟨═⟨⟩

You've reached middle age when all you exercise is caution.

UNKNOWN

⟨⟨═⟨⟩

The secret of staying young is to live honestly, eat slowly, and lie about your age.

LUCILLE BALL

Part of the secret of success in life is to eat what you like
and let the food fight it out inside.

MARK TWAIN

Our language is funny—a fat chance and slim chance are
the same thing.

J. GUSTAV WHITE

The only exercise some people get is jumping to con-
clusions . . .

BAPTIST COURIER

If America men are obsessed with money, American
women are obsessed with weight. The men talk of gain,
the women of loss, and I do not know which talk is the
more boring.

MARYA MANNES

Under this flabby exterior is an enormous lack of character.

OSCAR LEVANT

My advice to you is not to inquire why or whither, but just enjoy your ice cream while it's on your plate.

THORNTON WILDER

I like long walks, especially when they are taken by people who annoy me.
FRED ALLEN

It has been my experience that folks who have no vices have very few virtues.
ABRAHAM LINCOLN

When the stomach is full it is easy to talk of fasting.
ST. JEROME

There is no exercise better for the heart than reaching down and lifting people up.
JOHN ANDREW HOLMER

Hearty laughter is a good way to jog internally without having to go outdoors.

NORMAN COUSINS

Laziness is nothing more than the habit of resting before you get tired.
JULES RENARD

Exercise is a modern superstition, invented by people who ate too much, and had nothing to think about.
GEORGE SANTAYANA

I never take any exercise—except for breathing.
MARY GARDEN

Whenever I feel like exercise I lie down until the feeling passes.
ROBERT MAYNARD HUTCHINS

I have never taken any exercise, except for sleeping and resting, and I never intend to take any. Exercise is loathsome.

MARK TWAIN

Start slow and taper off.
WALT STACK

At six A.M. I always feel I should be up and doing something productive.
ARNOLD SCHWARZENEGGER

I am inclined to believe that the beneficent effects of the regular quarter-hour's exercise before breakfast is more than offset by the mental wear and tear in getting out of bed fifteen minutes earlier than one otherwise would.
SIMEON STRUNSKY

If you have to work before breakfast, get your breakfast first.
JOSH BILLINGS

I do not miss a day. It keeps me in check—bench pressing three hundred pounds will always be bench pressing three hundred pounds. That will never change, no matter how much money I have or how famous I am.

ARNOLD SCHWARZENEGGER

◖—◗

A diet is a plan, generally hopeless, for reducing your weight, which tests your will power but does little for your waistline.

HERBERT B. PROCHNOW

◖—◗

Exercise is the most awful illusion. The secret is a lot of aspirin and marrons glacés.

NOËL COWARD

◖—◗

How beautiful it is to do nothing, and then rest afterward.

SPANISH PROVERB

Our own physical body possesses a wisdom which we who inhabit the body lack. We give it orders which make no sense.

HENRY MILLER

I consider exercise vulgar. It makes people smell.

ALEC YUIK THORNTON

Any workout which does not involve a certain minimum of danger of responsibility does not improve the body— it just wears it out.

NORMAN MAILER

I don't jog. If I die I want to be sick.

ABE LEMONS

I get my exercise acting as a pallbearer to my friends who exercise.

CHAUNCEY DEPEW

Health nuts are going to feel stupid someday, lying in hospitals dying of nothing.

REDD FOXX

Early to rise and early to bed
Makes a male healthy, wealthy and dead.

JAMES THURBER

Life is one long process of getting tired.

SAMUEL BUTLER

I refuse to spend my life worrying about what I eat. There is no pleasure worth forgoing just for an extra three years in the geriatric ward.

JOHN MORTIMER

Be careful about reading health books. You may die of a misprint.

MARK TWAIN

Violent exercise is like a cold shower: you think it does you good because you feel better when you stop.

ROBERT QUILLEN

It makes people nervous to see someone running. I know that when I see someone running on my street, my instincts tell me to let the dog out after him.

MIKE ROYKO

Avoid running at all times.

SATCHEL PAIGE

Running is an unnatural act, except from enemies and to the bathroom.

UNKNOWN

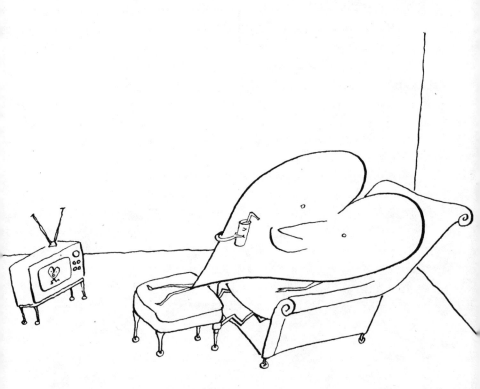

I believe every human has a finite number of heartbeats.
I don't intend to waste any of mine running around doing
exercises.

NEIL ARMSTRONG

Exercise is bunk. If you are healthy, you don't need it; if you are sick, you shouldn't take it.
HENRY FORD

All life is six to five against.
DAMON RUNYON

Exercise is the yuppie version of bulimia.
BARBARA EHRENREICH

The only reason I would take up jogging is so that I could hear heavy breathing again.
ERMA BOMBECK

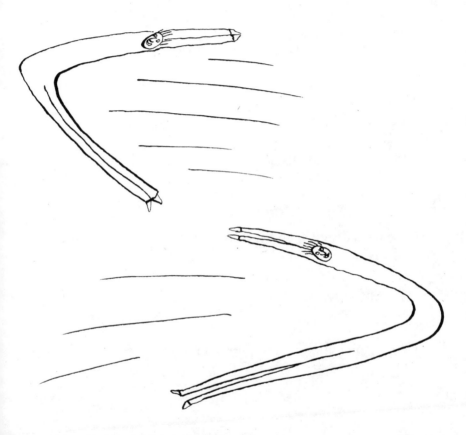

It's all right letting yourself go as long as you can let yourself back.

MICK JAGGER

If only it was as easy to banish hunger by rubbing the belly as it is to masturbate.

DIOGENES THE CYNIC

Θ—Θ

The right diet directs sexual energy into the parts that matter.

BARBARA CARTLAND

Θ—Θ

Give me a dozen such heartbreaks if that would help me lose a couple of pounds.

COLETTE

Θ—Θ

I see no objection to stoutness in moderation.

W.S. GILBERT

Θ—Θ

The reason fat people are happy is that the nerves are well protected.

LUCIANO PAVAROTTI

Gluttony is not a secret vice.
ORSON WELLES

Observe your dog: if he's fat you're not getting enough exercise.
EVAN ESAR

I have gained and lost the same ten pounds so many times over and over again my cellulite must have déjà vu.
JANE WAGNER

You know you've reached middle age when your weightlifting consists of merely standing up.
BOB HOPE

The best measure of a man's honesty isn't his income tax return. It's the zero adjustment on his bathroom scale.
ARTHUR C. CLARKE

Most people I know, given the choice of public flogging or public weighing, would choose the flogging.
STEPHEN PHILLIPS

Your body is the baggage you must carry through life. The more excess baggage, the shorter the trip.
ARNOLD GLASGOW

The belly overreaches the head.
FRENCH PROVERB

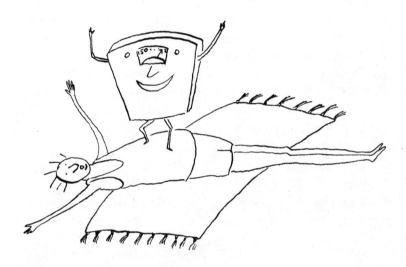

In the Middle Ages, they had guillotines, stretch racks, whips and chains. Nowadays, we have a much more effective torture device called the bathroom scale.
STEPHEN PHILLIPS

I go up and down the scale so often that if they ever perform an autopsy on me they'll find me like a strip of bacon—a streak of lean and a streak of fat.

TEXAS GUINAN

Where the guests at a gathering are well-acquainted, they eat twenty percent more than they otherwise would.

EDGAR WATSON HOWE

It is a hard matter, my fellow citizens, to argue with the belly, since it has no ears.

PLUTARCH

I'm allergic to food. Every time I eat it breaks out in fat.

JENNIFER GREENE DUNCAN

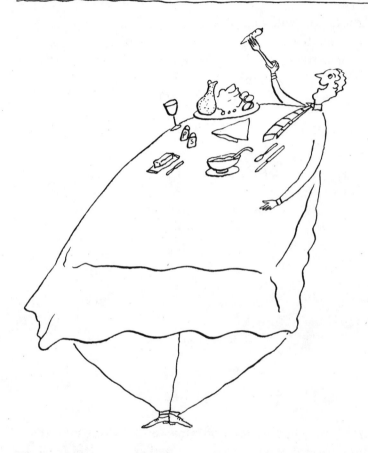

He had a paunch so big that he had to lean backwards just to stand up.

JIM BISHOP

Americans will eat garbage, provided you sprinkle it
liberally with ketchup, mustard, chili sauce, Tabasco
sauce, cayenne pepper, or any other condiment which
destroys the original flavor of the dish.

HENRY MILLER

I am a great eater of beef, and I believe that does harm to
my wit.

WILLIAM SHAKESPEARE
(TWELFTH NIGHT)

You are what you eat. For example, if you eat garlic you're
apt to be a hermit.

FRANKLIN P. JONES

Drinking when we are not thirsty and making love at any
time madame: that is all there is to distinguish us from the
animals.

PIERRE AGUSTIN DE BEAUMARCHAIS

Man is the only animal that can remain on friendly terms
with the victims he intends to eat until he eats them.
SAMUEL BUTLER

To a man with an empty stomach food is God.
               GANDHI

Preach not to others what they should eat, but eat as becomes you and be silent.
               EPICTETUS

While forbidden fruit is said to taste sweeter, it usually spoils faster.
           ABIGAIL VAN BUREN

Better a man should wait for a dish than a dish should wait for a man.
          CHINESE PROVERB

God sends meat and the devil sends cooks.
THOMAS DELONEY

Undoubtedly the desire for food has been and still is one of the main causes of political events.

BERTRAND RUSSELL

The most violent appetites of all creatures are lust and hunger: the first is a perpetual call upon them to propagate their kind, the latter to preserve themselves.

JOSEPH ADDISON

Never argue at the dinner table, for the one who is not hungry always gets the best of the argument.

RICHARD WHATELY

Hunger is not debatable.

HARRY HOPKINS

If you ask a hungry man how much is two and two, he replies four loaves.

HINDU PROVERB

Great eaters and great sleepers are incapable of anything else that is great.

HENRY IV OF FRANCE

Thought depends absolutely on the stomach, but in spite of that, those who have the best stomachs are not the best thinkers.

VOLTAIRE

I won't eat anything that has intelligent life, but I'd gladly eat a network executive or a politician.

MARTY FELDMAN

Is it progress if a cannibal uses a knife and fork?

STANISLAW LEM

A converted cannibal is one who, on Friday, eats only fishermen.

EMILY LOTNEY

Who ever heard of a fat man heading a riot, or herding together in turbulent mobs?

WASHINGTON IRVING

Better is a dinner of herbs where love is, than a fatted ox in the midst of hatred.

PROVERBS 15:17

I have known many meat eaters to be far more non-violent than vegetarians.

GANDHI

The first in banquets, but the last in fight.

HOMER

The waist is a terrible thing to mind.
ZIGGY

Fat is not a moral problem. It's an oral problem.
JANE THOMAS NOLAND

He that eats till he is sick must fast till he is well.
HEBREW PROVERB

Imprisoned in every fat man a thin one is wildly signal-
ling to be let out.
CYRIL CONNOLLY

People are the only animals who eat themselves to death.
AMA, JUNE 1971

Gluttony is an emotional escape, a sign something is eating us.

PETER DE VRIES

The body is a system of tubes and glands . . . a bundle of pipes and strainers, fitted to one another after so wonderful a manner as to make a proper engine for the soul to work with.

JOSEPH ADDISON

The belly is the reason why man does not mistake himself for a God.

FRIEDRICH NIETZSCHE

He who is a slave to the belly seldom worships God.

SAADI

The body is not a home but an inn—and that only briefly.

SENECA

The body never lies.

MARTHA GRAHAM

The sound body is the product of the sound mind.
GEORGE BERNARD SHAW

Why should a man's mind have been thrown into such close, sad, sensational, inexplicable relations with such a precarious object as his body?
THOMAS HARDY

The physically fit can enjoy their vices.
LLOYD PERCIVAL

Statistics show that of those who contract the habit of eating very few survive.
WALLACE IRWIN

Clogged with yesterday's excess, the body drags the mind down with it.

HORACE

If you knew how your dinner was made, you'd lose your lunch.

PEOPLE FOR THE ETHICAL TREATMENT OF ANIMALS

Don't eat anything that has a face. Don't eat anything that has sexual urges, that has a mother and father or that tries to run away from you.

JOHN ROBBINS

It's all right to drink like a fish—if you drink what a fish drinks.

MARY PETTIBONE POOLE

We never repent of having eaten too little.

THOMAS JEFFERSON

The dinosaur's eloquent lesson is that if some bigness is good, an overabundance of bigness is not necessarily better.

ERIC JOHNSTON

There is more to life than increasing its speed.

GANDHI

He who distinguishes the true savor of his food can never be a glutton; he who does not cannot be otherwise.

THOREAU

Oh that this too too solid flesh would melt, thaw and resolve itself into a dew.

WILLIAM SHAKESPEARE
(*HAMLET*)

The one way to get thin is to re-establish a purpose in life.
CYRIL CONNOLLY

Eat before shopping. If you go to the store hungry, you are likely to make unnecessary purchases.
AMERICAN HEART ASSOCIATION COOKBOOK

It isn't so much what's on the table that matters, as what's on the chairs.
W. S. GILBERT

We load up on oat bran in the morning so we'll live forever. Then we spend the rest of the day living like there's no tomorrow.
LEE IACOCCA

Remember you're all alone in the kitchen, and no one can see you.

JULIA CHILD

The appetite grows by eating.

RABELAIS

The boa constrictor, when he has had an adequate meal, goes to sleep, and does not wake until he needs another meal. Human beings, for the most part, are not like this.

BERTRAND RUSSELL

Hunger is the best sauce in the world.

CERVANTES

If a fly gets into the throat of one who is fasting, it is not necessary to pull it out.

AYATOLLAH KHOMENI

The toughest part of being on a diet is shutting up about it.
GERALD NACHMAN

Life itself is the proper binge.
JULIA CHILD

Enough is as good as a feast.
JOHN HEYWOOD

Do not bite at the bait of pleasure till you know there is no hook beneath it.
THOMAS JEFFERSON

Food is an important part of a balanced diet.
FRAN LEBOWITZ

Cooking is love—it should be entered into with abandon, or not at all.

HARRIET VAN HORNE

Anyone who eats three meals a day should understand why cookbooks outsell sex books, three to one.

L. M. BOYD

Love: A word properly applied to our delight in particular kinds of food; sometimes metaphorically spoken of the favorite objects of all our appetites.

HENRY FIELDING

Never eat more than you can lift.

MISS PIGGY

Grub first, then ethics.

BERTOLT BRECHT

Strange to see how a good dinner and feasting reconciles everybody.

SAMUEL PEPYS

After a good dinner, one can forgive anybody, even one's own relations.

OSCAR WILDE

To eat is human
To digest divine

MARK TWAIN

There is no love sincerer than the love of food.
GEORGE BERNARD SHAW

A man may be a pessimistic determinist before lunch and an optimistic believer in the will's freedom after it.

ALDOUS HUXLEY

I have a simple philosophy. Fill what's empty. Empty what's full. And scratch where it itches.

ALICE LONGWORTH ROOSEVELT

A man is in general better pleased when he has a good dinner upon his table, than when his wife talks Greek.

SAMUEL JOHNSON

To as great a degree as sexuality, food is inseparable from imagination.

JEAN-FRANÇOIS REVEL

Too much of a good thing can be wonderful.
MAE WEST

Security is a smile from a headwaiter.
RUSSELL BAKER

When those waiters ask me if I want some fresh ground pepper, I ask if they have any aged pepper.
ANDY ROONEY

Poets have been mysteriously silent on the subject of cheese.
G. K. CHESTERTON

The noblest of all dogs is the hot-dog: it feeds the hand that bites it.
LAURENCE J. PETER

Cheese—milk's leap toward immortality.
CLIFTON FADIMAN

If men ate soufflé before meetings, life could be much different.

JACQUES BAEYENS

What is patriotism but the love of the good things we ate in our childhood?

LIN YUTANG

You first parents of the human race . . . who ruined yourself for an apple, what might you not have done for a truffled turkey?

JEAN ANTHELME BRILLAT-SAVARIN

I would eat my own father with such a sauce.
GRIMOD DE LA REYNIERE

I refuse to believe that trading recipes is silly. Tuna-fish casserole is at least as real as corporate stock.

BARBARA GRIZZUTI HARRISON

Seeing isn't believing, it's eating that's believing.

JAMES THURBER

Gastronomical perfection can be reached in these combinations: one person dining alone, usually upon a couch or a hillside; two persons, of no matter what sex or age, dining in a good restaurant; six people of no matter what sex or age, dining in a good home.

M. F. K. FISHER

Great food is like great sex—the more you have the more you want.

GAEL GREENE

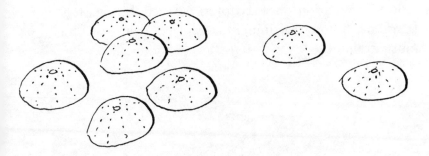

Success to me is having ten honeydew melons and eating only the top half of each one.

BARBRA STREISAND

Dinnertime is the most wonderful period of the day and perhaps its goal—the blossoming of the day. Breakfast is the bud.

NOVALIS

All happiness depends on a leisurely breakfast.

JOHN GUNTHER

A dinner invitation, once accepted, is a sacred obligation. If you die before the dinner takes place, your executor must attend.

WARD MCALLISTER

Life, within doors, has few pleasanter prospects than a neatly arranged and well-provisioned breakfast table.

NATHANIEL HAWTHORNE

The discovery of a new dish does more for the happiness
of mankind than the discovery of a new star.
JEAN ANTHELME BRILLAT-SAVARIN

All history attests
That happiness for man—the hungry sinner—
Since Eve ate apples,
Much depends on dinner!
GEORGE GORDON, LORD BYRON

Americans are just beginning to regard food the way the French always have. Dinner is not what you do in the evening before something else. Dinner is the evening.
ART BUCHWALD

I never eat when I can dine.
MAURICE CHEVALIER

Everything ends this way in France—everything. Wed-
dings, christenings, duels, burials, swindlings, diplo-
matic affairs—everything is a pretext for a good dinner.
JEAN ANOUILH

A good eater must be a good man; for a good eater must have a good digestion, and a good digestion depends upon a good conscience.

BENJAMIN DISRAELI

The halls of the professor and the philosopher are deserted, but what a crowd there is in the cafés.

LUCIUS ANNAEUS SENECA

There is more simplicity in the man who eats caviar on impulse than in the man who eats grapenuts on principle.

G. K. CHESTERTON

I like the philosophy of the *sandwich*, as it were. It typifies my attitude to life, really. It's all there, it's fun, it looks good, and you don't have to wash up afterwards.

MOLLY PARKIN

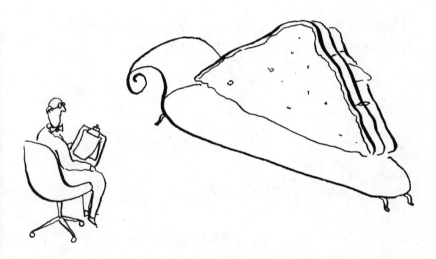

Too few people understand a really good sandwich.
JAMES BEARD

I doubt the world holds for anyone a more soul-stirring surprise than the first adventure with ice cream.

HEYWOOD BROUN

If there is anything we Chinese are serious about, it is neither religion nor learning, but food.

LIN YUTANG

Where you eat is sacred.

MEL BROOKS

What is a roofless cathedral compared to a well-built pie?

WILLIAM MAGINN

When one has tasted watermelon he knows what the angels eat.

MARK TWAIN

Plain cooking cannot be entrusted to plain cooks.
COUNTESS MORPHY

No mean woman can cook well, for it calls for a light head, a generous spirit, and a large heart.
PAUL GAUGUIN

A good cook is like a sorceress who dispenses happiness.
ELSA SCHIAPARELLI

Let the salad-maker be a spendthrift for oil, a miser for vinegar, a statesman for salt and a madman for mixing.
SPANISH PROVERB

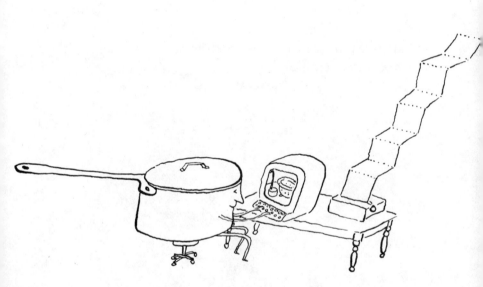

Progress in civilization has been accompanied by progress in cookery.

FANNIE FARMER

It requires a certain kind of mind to see beauty in a hamburger bun.

RAY KROC

I hate television. I hate it as much as peanuts. But I can't stop eating peanuts.

ORSON WELLES

I come from a home where gravy is a beverage.

ERMA BOMBECK

Poultry is for the cook what canvas is for the painter.

JEAN ANTHELME BRILLAT-SAVARIN

Cauliflower is nothing but cabbage with a college education.
MARK TWAIN

A first-rate soup is more creative than a second-rate painting.

ABRAHAM MASLOW

My good health is due to a soup made of white doves. It is simply wonderful.

MADAME CHIANG KAI-SHEK

Of soup and love, the first is best.

SPANISH PROVERB

I live on good soup, not fine words.

MOLIÈRE

Chowder breathes reassurance. It steams consolation.
CLEMENTINE PADDLEFORD

What I say is that, if a man really likes potatoes, he must be a pretty decent sort of fellow.

A. A. MILNE

Talk of joy: there may be things better than beef stew and baked potatoes and home-made bread—there may be.

DAVID GRAYSON

Pray for peace and grace and spiritual food,
For wisdom and guidance, for all these are good,
But don't forget the potatoes.

JOHN TYLER PETEE

My idea of heaven is a great big baked potato and someone to share it with.

OPRAH WINFREY

Eggs for an hour, bread of a day, wine of a year, a friend of thirty years.

ITALIAN PROVERB

How simple and frugal a thing is happiness: a glass of wine, a roast chestnut, a wretched little brazier, the sound of the sea . . .

NIKOS KAZANTZAKIS

Wine is sure proof that God loves us and wants us to be happy.

BENJAMIN FRANKLIN

Only Irish coffee provides in a single glass all four essential food groups: alcohol, caffeine, sugar, and fat.

ALEX LEVINE

Nothing ever tasted better than a cold beer on a beautiful afternoon with nothing to look forward to but more of the same.

HUGH HOOD

Lettuce is like conversation: it must be fresh and crisp, and so sparkling that you scarcely notice the bitter in it.
CHARLES DUDLEY WARNER

What was paradise, but a garden full of vegetables and herbs and pleasures. Nothing there but delights.
WILLIAM LAWSON

Happy is said to be the family which can eat onions together. They are, for the time being, separate from the world, and have a harmony of aspiration.
CHARLES DUDLEY WARNER

I do not know of a flowering plant that tastes good and is poisonous. Nature is not out to get you.
EUELL GIBBONS

The green and gold of my delight—
Asparagus with Hollandaise.

THOMAS AUGUSTINE DALY

In a restaurant choose a table near a waiter.
JEWISH FOLK SAYING

Without bread, without wine, love is nothing.
FRENCH PROVERB

Even were a cook to cook a fly, he would keep the breast
for himself.
POLISH PROVERB

Worries go down better with soup.
YIDDISH PROVERB

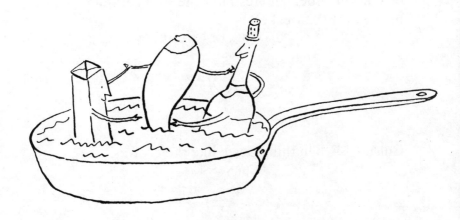

Fish, to taste right, must swim three times—in water, in
butter and in wine in the stomach.
                    POLISH PROVERB

Seasoning is in Cookery what chords are in music.
LOUIS EUSTACHE UDE

Salt is the policeman of taste: it keeps the various flavors of a dish in order, and restrains the stronger from tyrannizing over the weaker.
MALCOLM DE CHAZAL

Cuisine is when things taste like themselves.
CURNONSKY

I believe that if ever I had to practice cannibalism, I might manage if there were enough tarragon around.
JAMES BEARD

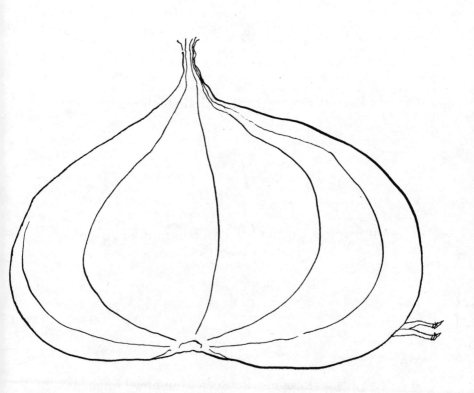

There is no such thing as a little garlic.
ALFRED BAER

No man is lonely while eating spaghetti.
ROBERT MORLEY

If I can't have too many truffles I'll do without.
COLETTE

I think if I were a woman I'd wear coffee as a perfume.
JOHN VAN DRUTEN

So far I've always kept my diet secret but now I might as well tell everyone what it is. Lots of grapefruit throughout the day and plenty of virile young men.
ANGIE DICKINSON

Everything you / see I owe to spaghetti.
SOPHIA LOREN

If there were no such thing as eating, we should have to invent it to save man from despairing.

DR. WILHELM STEKHEL

Some people have food, but no appetite. Others have appetite, but no food. I have both—the Lord be praised.

OLIVER CROMWELL

Nothing would be more tiresome than eating and drinking if God had not made them a pleasure as well as a necessity.

VOLTAIRE

Eating takes a special talent. Some people are much better at it than others. In that way, it's like sex, and as with sex, it's more fun with someone who really likes it. I can't imagine having a lasting friendship with anyone who is not interested in food.

ALAN KING

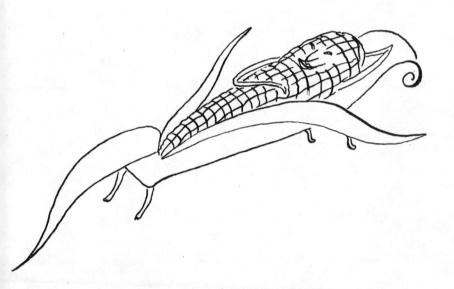

Sex is good, but not as good as fresh sweet corn.
GARRISON KEILLOR